LOVING LIFE

KEY TO ENJOYING EVERYDAY

OBIORA EZE

CONTENTS

INTRODUCTION

Not long ago, a tragic event occurred in my neighborhood: a young boy took his own life. This story deeply affected me because I once felt so hopeless and sad that I thought about doing the same thing. Back then, life seemed completely worthless and joyless. Now, when I think about those times, the reasons for my despair seem small because I understand life better.

Sadly, this young boy's story is not uncommon. Our world is full of challenges and fears, and more people, especially young ones, are becoming depressed. Many feel alone and scared, and life feels like something to endure rather than enjoy. People often seek help from professionals, but the relief they find doesn't last because it doesn't get to the heart of the problem: a lack of peace.

True peace means feeling calm and sure that everything is okay. It's like how things were at the beginning of time when everything was perfect and there were no troubles. But when humans lost their connection to the source of life—the force that created everything—they also lost this peace. Ever since, despite trying many different ways, we haven't been able to get it back.

Life changes constantly, which can make us feel more worried, stressed, and sad. This affects how we treat each other. Even with all our modern advancements, people still struggle to live together in harmony. Relationships end, businesses fail, and communities suffer—all because we can't find true peace. Some groups and religions have tried to bring peace through certain practices or thoughts, but these attempts have only provided temporary solutions.

Martin Luther King Jr. once said that even though we can do incredible things like flying or swimming like fish, we still haven't learned how to live together peacefully. He meant that understanding life deeply is the key to real peace. If we don't understand the purpose of life, we misuse it. Knowing life well brings peace to ourselves, and then to others. If we aren't at peace with ourselves, it's hard to be at peace with anyone else.

The main issue is that people have lost their connection to the source of life, and that's why there's so much unrest and conflict. "Loving Life: The Key to Enjoying Everyday" is about finding that connection again. It's about learning how to find real happiness and joy, both within ourselves and with others. This book will discuss what life really means, what matters most, and how best to live. Let's embark on this journey to not just love life, but to truly live it to the fullest.

PART ONE

UNDERSTANDING LIFE

CHAPTER 1- WHAT IS LIFE?

At some point in life, we all find ourselves pausing to question our existence. "Why am I here?" "What comes next after achieving all my goals?" These questions often arise as we transition from childhood, through adulthood, to old age—constantly engaged in activities aiming towards a goal. But what exactly is this ultimate goal?

King Solomon, often celebrated as one of the richest and wisest kings of ancient Israel, pondered these very questions during his reign from 970 to 931 BCE. In his quest for understanding, Solomon embarked on an extensive exploration of life's earthly pleasures and achievements. His conclusion was stark: "Everything is vanity."

The book of Ecclesiastes vividly captures Solomon's grand experiments with pleasure and wealth:

"I made great works; built houses; planted vineyards; created gardens and parks, planting all kinds of fruit trees. I made pools of water to irrigate the flourishing forest. I bought slaves—both men and women—and had my own servants. I owned more herds and flocks than anyone in Jerusalem before me. I amassed silver and gold, the treasure of kings and provinces. I acquired male and female singers and all the luxuries a man could desire. And yet, when I surveyed all that my hands had done and what I had toiled to achieve, everything was meaningless—a chasing after the wind; there was no value in any of it under the sun." (Ecclesiastes 2:4-11 ASV)

To someone who has not yet achieved all conceivable ambitions, Solomon's words might seem abstract, even unrelatable. The common belief is that our pursuits are meant to keep us contentedly busy. However, Solomon achieved it all—wealth, pleasure, even a staggering number of 700 wives and 300 concubines. Yet, he descended into despair.

This pattern isn't just a relic of ancient times; it's evident in modern societies too. In many developed nations, despite extensive social safety nets, depression rates are climbing, mirroring Solomon's discontent. This begs the question: if not in these achievements and pleasures, where does the essence of life truly lie?

The answer lies not in what life offers—its material abundance and fleeting joys—but in understanding the deeper objectives and purposes for which it was created. Life's true meaning is found not in its gifts but in its intentions and the fulfillment they bring.

Life And Its Provisions

To fully appreciate life, it is crucial to distinguish between the essence of life itself and the provisions it offers. Consider the example of a grand pipe organ. With its majestic form and artfully crafted pipes, it is indeed a visual marvel. One might be tempted to further enhance its appearance—painting, adorning, and sealing its pipes to transform it into a stunning showpiece. However, this would neglect its true purpose: to produce music. The organ's design serves not merely for admiration but as a conduit for melody, its real essence.

Similarly, the luxurious interiors of an airplane can captivate us, yet if the plane never takes flight, it is merely an expensive artifact, its potential wasted. This situation parallels how many people experience life—mesmerized by its physical offerings, yet not truly engaging with life itself. We become enthralled with the "decorations" of life—the material and superficial aspects—without tapping into the core of living. To live is to unleash life's potential, not merely to exist within its boundaries.

This common misunderstanding significantly misaligns us from our true purpose. Just as the pipe organ is intended to produce harmonies and the airplane to soar, each individual is equipped with unique abilities and a profound mission that surpasses simple survival and sensory satisfaction. Life, in its most genuine form, involves creating, experiencing, and contributing—it's not solely about accumulation and admiration.

When our focus is solely on life's provisions— the tangible assets, the public recognition, and the physical pleasures—we limit ourselves to a superficial understanding of what it means to exist. It is akin to observing the brushstrokes on a canvas and mistaking them for the artwork itself, without grasping the narrative it conveys or the emotions it arouses. These elements are designed to support and enrich our journey through life, not to define it. By embracing this broader perspective, we can align more closely with life's true intentions and fulfill our deepest potential.

Understanding The Blueprint Of Life

To truly grasp the essence of life, we must start with a foundation of sincerity and aim our search toward its origin. The age-old question "What is life?" has puzzled philosophers, scholars, and spiritual seekers for centuries. Often, this quest leads to confusion when the answers sought are detached from the concept of creation and its Creator. Life, fundamentally, is more than the sum of its parts —it's the manifestation of divine intentionality, a precious gift from the Creator designed to be cherished, nurtured, and respected.

Deviation from this divine-centered perspective leads us into a void where life appears as nothing more than a series of fleeting moments and superficial achievements. To truly understand life's purpose, we must see it as a purposeful creation, not a series of random events. This understanding requires us to consider the intentions of the Creator, akin to understanding the mind behind a blueprint. Neglecting the role of the Creator is like denying the existence of a design, which implies that life is merely chaotic and purposeless.

Interestingly, even those who deny the existence of a creator live their lives according to a set pattern, suggesting an intrinsic acknowledgment of design. They leave their homes with the intention of returning, their daily routines subtly affirming the existence of a purposeful design. If life were truly accidental, their actions and outcomes would be as unpredictable as the wind. This contradiction highlights the wisdom in acknowledging a creator's role, as suggested by Proverbs 14:1, which points out the folly of overlooking the divine hand in the fabric of existence. To reject the notion of a creator is to dismiss the very basis of order and purpose in our universe.

Embracing Life's Intentional Design

To find true meaning in life, we must explore its intentional design and seek insights from the Creator. This journey is not about conforming to religious norms but about recognizing that the universe is structured with purpose and connecting with the intelligence behind it. Acknowledging this not only enhances our understanding of our roles but also fosters respect for the intricate design that links all life forms. By embracing this perspective, we honor our lives and contribute to the coherence and significance of the vast, mysterious journey of existence.

Beyond Temporary Pleasures

Life is often mistakenly defined by the pursuit of wealth, pleasure, or societal status. These aspects, while satisfying in the moment, do not provide lasting happiness or a deep sense of purpose. The true essence and joy of life transcend these ephemeral gains, it is found fundamentally in:

1. **Our Connection to the Divine:** This involves recognizing and deepening our relationship with a higher power, which offers a profound sense of peace and purpose beyond the material world.

2. **Expression of Our Unique Talents and Purposes:** Each person is endowed with specific gifts. Real fulfillment comes from using these talents to impact the world positively, aligning our actions with our true purposes.

3. **Contributions to Our Communities and Beyond:** Life's value is greatly enhanced when we contribute meaningfully to the communities we are part of, fostering improvements and championing collective well-being.

The narrative of Adam in the Book of Genesis illuminates the initial intentions for humanity. Positioned in a verdant garden, Adam was tasked with stewardship and creativity, living in direct communion with the Creator. His life was characterized by a harmonious existence with nature and was focused on fulfilling divine intentions, not self-centered goals. This harmonious state highlights the core essence of life —living aligned with the purpose for which we were created, continuously manifesting and reflecting the divine nature.

"So God created man in his own image, in the image of God created he him; male and female created he them." (Genesis 1:27 KJV)

The Fall And Redemption

Humanity's journey has significantly strayed from its foundational blueprint due to the Fall, which severed the intrinsic connection to our divine purpose. As a result, modern life is often viewed through the lenses of individualism and materialism, with a heavy emphasis on short-lived pleasures. However, the teachings and life of Jesus Christ provide a blueprint for returning to life's true essence. He lived as a beacon of service, community, and divine connection—attributes that define a life fulfilled according to the original design.

"In Him was life, and that life was the light of men." (John 1:4) Jesus demonstrated the ultimate expression of divine purpose through His miracles, teachings, and His ultimate sacrifice—death and subsequent resurrection. His life serves as a powerful testament to the potential within us all to overcome our limitations and live fully in the design crafted for us by the Creator.

Emulating The Divine Blueprint

Following Jesus' example allows us to break free from the shackles of mundane existence and rediscover the richness of life intended from the beginning. This pathway is not about adhering to rigid dogmas but about engaging with the structured, purposeful universe the Creator has ordained. In doing so, we honor our role in this vast, interconnected tapestry of existence and contribute to a world that reflects divine principles of order, purpose, and holistic living.

Embracing this understanding urges us to not only live life but to live it abundantly, with every action and decision woven into the broader narrative of divine intention. This perspective reshapes our daily experiences, guiding us toward a life that is not just survived, but richly and meaningfully lived.

CHAPTER 2 - LIFE AND IT'S CHALLENGES

The journey of life is often interpreted through the difficulties we encounter, leading many to measure their life's worth by the challenges they face. However, this view overlooks the profound wisdom found in the scriptures, particularly highlighted in the Book of Genesis. The opening verses (Genesis 1:1-3) convey that challenges should not be seen as indicators of life's deficiencies but as opportunities to wield the authority and wisdom endowed by our Creator.

"In the beginning God created the heaven and the earth. And the earth was without form, and void; and darkness was upon the face of the deep. And the Spirit of God moved upon the face of the waters. And God said, 'Let there be light': and there was light." (Genesis

1:1-3 KJV)

This passage illustrates the earth's initial state of chaos and void, transformed into order and light by God's command. It teaches us that darkness and disorder are not permanent but can be overcome through divine intervention.

The True Nature Of Challenges

Scripture teaches us that challenges are natural elements of Earth's existence. They are not measures of life's worth but are instead natural conditions of our world that can be transformed through faith and wisdom. The misconception that life's value depends on the absence of challenges gives undue power to negativity and obscures the potential for growth and transformation.

Satan thrives on distortions, leading us to view challenges as insurmountable obstacles. He is described by Christ as the "father of lies," often weaving deception to make us falter through doubt and fear. However, an enlightened understanding recognizes that solutions lie within the truth and wisdom imparted by Jesus Christ.

Divine Strategy: Confronting Chaos With Hope

The divine response to chaos is not resignation but

active engagement through hope, faith, and love. Just as God created light from darkness, we are called to bring order from chaos and substance from void. This proactive approach underscores our responsibility to face challenges not with despair or resignation but with spiritual wisdom.

Learning From The Life Of Jesus Christ

Jesus Christ's life is a prime example of overcoming adversity. Born into poverty, without formal theological education, and belonging to a marginalized group, He faced immense challenges, including natural disasters and logistical dilemmas like feeding thousands with minimal resources. Yet, He consistently overcame these challenges through His spiritual connection with God, drawing on His divine sonship for courage and assurance.

His ultimate challenge—His crucifixion and subsequent resurrection—was met with the same divine confidence and guidance, illustrating the profound potential of faith to turn trials into triumphs.

Embracing Challenges As Opportunities

Understanding life's challenges in this light empowers us to adopt a perspective of empowerment rather than victimhood. It encourages us to see that the quality of life is determined not by the absence of difficulties but by our responses to them. By embracing our spiritual foundations and following Christ's example, we can transform our personal and collective adversities into opportunities for growth, creativity, and meaningful contribution. This empowered approach not only enhances our own lives but also contributes positively to those around us, spreading light where there was once darkness.

Spiritual Connection: Beyond Rituals

The ability to navigate life with purpose and clarity, as Jesus did, stems from a profound spiritual relationship with the Creator—a bond akin to that between a parent and their child. This connection goes beyond traditional religious practices, offering a direct and unmediated path to divine guidance and understanding. Jesus' life was marked by an intimate fellowship with God, allowing him to communicate with the Creator with ease and confidence. This type of relationship is not rooted in rituals or ceremonies, but in a deep spiritual unity with the Creator.

Harmonizing With The Creator's Nature

The concept of a spiritual connection emphasizes the importance of aligning with the Creator's essence. Communication is most effective between beings of similar nature. For Jesus, his spirit was in perfect alignment with God's, sharing the same divine identity. This deep congruence facilitated an exceptional level of communion and understanding, enabling Jesus to perfectly manifest God's qualities and will through his actions. True fellowship is possible when there is commonality, and in Christ's case, his shared nature with God made perfect fellowship achievable.

Cultivating Spiritual Kinship

To truly understand the design of life, we must foster a relationship with the Creator based on spiritual kinship rather than mere religious observance. It's about identifying with God and developing a personal connection that unlocks the divine spirit within us. This spiritual harmony allows us to comprehend our purpose and navigate life's complexities with wisdom and grace.

Accessing Divine Guidance

Embracing our spiritual identity is key to accessing the Creator's guidance and fulfilling His will in our lives. This connection empowers us to transcend the mundane aspects of existence and draws us closer to the core of our being and the ultimate purpose for our lives. In this spiritual journey, we find the strength to exhibit divine characteristics such as love, faith, and hope, thus reaching our highest potential and contributing to the Creator's plan in the world.

Living Out Our Divine Purpose

Life is not merely a pursuit of personal satisfaction through earthly achievements; it is a journey of rediscovering our divine purpose and potential. It involves living in a manner that reflects our unique contributions to the world, demonstrating the diverse aspects of God's nature through our actions, thoughts, and relationships. Each of us is a distinct expression of the divine, endowed with specific gifts, talents, and purposes that, when fully realized, enhance the creation's tapestry in unique ways.

To live is to express the divine nature within us, to fulfill our role in the greater story of creation, and to recognize our part in something much larger than ourselves. Life, in its truest form, is a sacred gift—an opportunity to partake in the unfolding of the divine plan on Earth. This insight carries with it the responsibility to live intentionally, aligned with the principles of love, faith, and hope that underpin the very fabric of life.

Life As A Divine Invitation

Life is not an exercise in vanity; it is a divine invitation to become co-creators in a reality that mirrors the beauty, diversity, and majesty of the Creator. The disconnection from God led to confusion and a loss of peace with oneself and with others. Reestablishing this connection restores peace within and extends it to our relationships with all of creation, inviting a harmonious existence that reflects our true spiritual heritage.

PART TWO

THE IMPORTANT THREE

CHAPTER 3-
LIVING BY HOPE

Hope serves as the guiding light through the stormy waters of life, much like a beacon that directs sailors through uncertain seas. Just as sailors trust their compass to navigate where the ocean meets the sky in a seemingly infinite horizon, we rely on hope to find our way. It goes beyond simple wishful thinking; hope is a deep-seated expectation for what is not yet seen but feels as real and vital as the heartbeat within us.

In our modern world, where shadows of negativity loom large—cast by distressing news cycles and a complex blend of genuine and perceived threats—hope is not just nice to have; it's essential. It is the very essence that sustains joy in life. Jesus Himself acknowledged the certainty of daily challenges in Matthew 6:34, but He also taught us that it is our hopeful outlook that reveals the beauty of each new day.

Armed with hope, we approach daily challenges not as barriers but as opportunities to enrich our lives with significance and potential. This hopeful perspective transforms every moment, allowing us to live fully and fearlessly, anchored by the promise of tomorrow.

The Essence Of Hope

Hope is not simply a passive longing for what the future might hold—it's an active engagement with possibilities yet unseen. Imagine it as being "impregnated" with the future, nurturing within ourselves the potential for what is yet to manifest. This dynamic conception of hope is like a gardener planting seeds with faith, attending them with love and patience, believing in the growth of plants unseen at the moment of sowing.

This powerful aspect of hope is not a human invention but a divine attribute. God Himself operates in the realm of hope, calling into existence things that are not, as when He said, "Let there be light." This wasn't just a command but a declaration of a reality He envisioned and brought forth, illustrating that to dream and to declare is to tap into God's creative authority.

Society, however, often peddles a lie that our lives are only as good as what we can see, touch, or measure right now. This illusion traps many in despair. Take, for example, someone who loses their job and sees this as an absolute end, believing their worth and their means to provide have vanished. This myopic view obscures the endless possibilities that extend beyond the current moment. If this person knew of potential opportunities ahead—like a future encounter leading to new work—would they still succumb to despair?

Hope is fundamentally rooted in our belief in a Creator—a benevolent force whose plans for us transcend the visible and immediate challenges we face. This belief instills in us a certainty that for every door that closes, a window opens somewhere, for those who keep faith. To say "there is no hope" is essentially to admit a blindness to this expansive spiritual reality.

Hope compels us to look beyond the immediate; it teaches us to see our lives as intricately designed by a Creator who makes all things possible for those who believe. By embracing hope, we view every setback not as a definitive end, but as a potential detour to new paths and brighter beginnings, all illuminated by the light of divine potential.

Therefore, hope is not merely wishful thinking but a strategic approach to life's challenges. It recognizes each difficulty as a redirection, an opportunity to explore alternative routes that might just be better than anything we imagined, all under the guidance of divine providence.

Hope As A Lifeline

In the vast desert of despair, hope is the oasis that keeps us going. Without it, life becomes a grueling journey through a barren landscape, devoid of comfort. When we rely only on the tangible—our homes, possessions, and relationships—we live precariously, as all these can disappear in an instant. Anchoring our hopes solely in the material world is like building on shifting sands.

Hope inspires us to look beyond our immediate struggles, to dream of a future that surpasses our present difficulties. It encourages us to adopt a vision so clear and vivid that it begins to take shape internally long before it manifests in the external world.

Transformative Encounters With Hope

I remember meeting a university student drowned in despair. He had turned to alcohol and frivolous spending to numb the pain of his depression, triggered by academic failures that seemed to shatter his dreams of graduating with honors. He believed all was lost. Through heartfelt discussions and prayer, he began to see the vast array of possibilities beyond his immediate troubles. Miraculously, a day after our conversation, a lecturer announced a correction in a grading error, which significantly boosted his marks. This news not only restored his joy but also reinforced the power of hope he was close to abandoning.

Hope In Popular Culture

The power of hope is not just a personal anecdote but is also vividly portrayed in popular culture. Mel Gibson's film "Apocalypto" depicts the protagonist, Jaguar Paw, whose unwavering hope and faith in his father's teachings, combined with his relentless desire to reunite with his family, drive him to overcome seemingly impossible odds. His story is a testament to the idea that a clear and firm vision can navigate us through the most formidable barriers.

Hope In Clinical Observations

The medical field also recognizes the crucial role of hope. Studies show that patients with a strong will to live often exhibit remarkable recoveries. Their hope seems to energize their bodies, enhancing their ability to fight illness. Conversely, those who succumb to despair typically face poorer outcomes. This resilience, powered by hope, demonstrates that our determination to persevere can change even the bleakest forecasts.

Hope, then, is more than just a metaphorical lifeline —it is a palpable force that can profoundly influence the direction of our lives, catalyze healing, and reshape our realities. It teaches us that our outlook on life—the way we view and respond to our challenges—has a profound impact on our overall experience. By embracing hope, we not only survive life's trials but transform them into opportunities for growth and renewal.

The Source Of True Hope

Many people place their hope in tangible things —wealth, relationships, status. However, these are transient and can dissolve like mist. Scripture clarifies that hope which is seen is hardly hope at all. True hope dwells in the unseen, in the eternal truths of God. It is anchored in His unchanging nature and in His promises, which are always fulfilled.

Hope acts as an anchor, and where this anchor is set makes all the difference. If it clasps onto solid rock, safety is assured; but if it latches onto rotting wood, collapse is inevitable. Thus, our hope must be grounded in the solid foundation of God's Word and His unshakable Kingdom. This hope is living and vibrant; it transcends temporary worldly conditions and secures us firmly in the everlasting.

True hope is not passive; it is dynamic and active. It requires us to engage deeply with our aspirations, to water these visions with faith, and to cultivate them with steadfast perseverance. Our minds are designed to shape our reality—the mental images we hold influence the outcomes we experience. These images form the expectations embedded within our subconscious, driven by our understanding of the natural laws as they apply to both the spiritual and physical realms.

Visualizing Hope Through God's Word

The mind constantly anticipates outcomes based on its inner visualizations. When these mental pictures are infused with the truth of God's Word, they are not only vivid but also reliable, backed by the Creator Himself. This divine visualization offers a "true picture" that goes beyond mere human expectation, providing a solid, trustworthy foundation for our hopes.

By rooting our hopes in God's eternal promises rather than the fleeting fixtures of the world, we anchor ourselves to a steadfast source of safety and truth. This spiritual anchoring not only sustains us through storms but also empowers us to thrive, transforming our inner visions into lived realities.

Living by hope means allowing the Holy Spirit to fill our hearts with divine aspirations, enabling us to collaborate with God in forging our destinies. It involves standing resolute in the midst of life's storms, firmly grasping God's promises, and trusting that the visions He has planted within us will undoubtedly manifest.

The Universality Of Hope

Hope is a powerful force that does not differentiate between sinners and saints; it is accessible to all who nurture it within their hearts. This truth is illustrated through the story of a friend I'll refer to as Jane. After completing her education, Jane secured a promising job and was enjoying her youthful exuberance. Her life took an unexpected turn when she discovered she was pregnant. The joy of potential motherhood was overshadowed by fear, fueled by daunting stories of childbirth from her family and the abandonment by her boyfriend who refused to accept fatherhood.

Amidst societal pressures to terminate the pregnancy, Jane found solace in a faith-based book that depicted Christ's crucifixion, emphasizing that He had borne our physical and emotional pains. Inspired by this, Jane turned to prayer, entrusting her fears and hopes for a painless childbirth to Jesus. Her faith was a beacon that cut through her fear; when the time came, she experienced a remarkably smooth delivery, affirming the power of the hope she had clung to. This experience was not only transformative for Jane but also reinforced by the unexpected support from her friends and colleagues.

The Parable Of The Pregnant Deer

The story of a pregnant deer trapped in a perilous predicament further underscores the potency of hope. Encircled by a raging forest fire, a predatory lion, and a hunter poised to strike, the deer found herself at a river, a precarious sanctuary fraught with crocodiles. Confronted with seemingly insurmountable threats on all sides, she focused singularly on drinking water — a basic act of sustaining life. In the moments that followed, a flash of lightning caused the hunter to misfire, striking the lion instead. This fortuitous event, coupled with a sudden downpour that extinguished the fire, provided the deer a chance to escape and eventually give birth safely. This narrative captures the essence of hope: when embraced, it can miraculously shift circumstances in our favor.

Embracing And Declaring Hope

These stories teach us the transformative and life-affirming power of hope. They encourage us to dream big, to cast our visions far beyond the constraints of our current realities. We are called to declare these visions not as far-off dreams but as imminent realities, drawing upon our faith that in partnership with God, all things are possible.

As we journey through life, our hope should shine as a testament to God's eternal truth. It should illuminate paths for those wandering in the shadows of doubt and despair, showcasing the undeniable strength that faith in God's promises provides. Hope does not merely help us endure; it empowers us to thrive, ensuring that despite the challenges we face, we can approach each day with courage and the assurance that for those who love God and align with His divine purpose, all things will indeed work together for good.

In nurturing hope, we not only bolster our own resilience but also inspire others to believe in the prospect of a brighter future. Let us then carry this beacon of hope forward, spreading its light and warmth to all corners of our lives and beyond.

CHAPTER 4- LIVING BY FAITH

I n the intricate tapestry of life, faith acts as the golden thread, weaving through every experience and challenge, binding our hopes to the reality of what we cannot yet see. It is the robust foundation upon which we construct our dreams, providing the assurance that what we desire is not only possible but has been preordained in the spiritual realm, simply awaiting its manifestation in our lives.

This chapter explores how living by faith is not merely a passive state of mind but an active force that shapes how we view our world and motivates us toward our divine destinies. As we delve deeper, we will see how faith sustains us, not just in times of tranquility, but more importantly, in moments of uncertainty.

The Nature Of Faith

Faith transcends simple belief; it is the very substance of things hoped for, the proof of realities that remain unseen (Hebrews 11:1). This proof doesn't reside in the tangible, physical world but emerges from the promises of God. As we delve into His Word, we find a firm foundation for our trust —this becomes the bedrock upon which our hopes are anchored. His promises are not just words; they are the tangible evidence that what we hope for will indeed come to fruition. Thus, faith and hope are intertwined; faith acts as the concrete evidence needed to substantiate our hopes, affirming their reality.

Manifestation Of Spiritual Blessings

The Creator has endowed us with abundant provisions that, while not physical, are immensely rich and accessible only through spiritual discernment.

"Blessed be the God and Father of our Lord Jesus Christ, who hath blessed us with all spiritual blessings in heavenly places in Christ." (Ephesians 1:3 KJV)

These blessings are spiritual and located in the heavenly realms, connected to us through Christ.

This concept isn't a novelty; it echoes the foundational act of creation itself. God manifested the visible universe from the invisible, a truth encapsulated in the Scriptures:

"Through faith we understand that the worlds were framed by the word of God, so that things which are seen were not made out of things which do appear." (Hebrews 11:3 KJV)

"(As it is written, I have made thee a father of many nations,) before him whom he believed, even God, who quickeneth the dead, and calleth those things which be not as though they were." (Romans 4:17 KJV)

Just as God said, "Let there be light," He brought forth light from a non-physical reality based on the divine blueprint He envisioned. When we speak something into existence, like declaring "let there be a table," it stems from a mental image or blueprint of the table. Similarly, God possessed a blueprint of everything He created, which Apostle Paul refers to as "the heavenly."

Created in His image, we too are endowed with the divine capability to manifest the intangible into the tangible. As His children, we are called to continue this creative work, bringing forth great works from the supernatural into our natural, physical world. This divine process of calling forth that which does not yet exist into reality is not only our inheritance but our duty as co-creators with Christ.

Protocols Of Manifestation

The process by which God manifested the invisible into the visible offers us a blueprint for bringing our own visions to life. This divine example delineates specific steps crucial for the manifestation of faith.

1. Vision: Initially, the Creator possessed a clear and distinct vision—an invisible picture of what He intended to create and where it would take form. This vision was precise and detailed, encompassing not just the outcome but the essence and placement of His creation.

2. Utterance: God then spoke His vision into existence. This wasn't merely speaking; it was a powerful decree that engaged divine forces to actualize what He envisioned. His words were not idle but charged with the power of the Holy Spirit, ensuring that what was spoken would indeed materialize.

3. Concurring Action: The manifestation might have involved time, though the exact duration is beyond our knowing since God operates from eternity but interacts within time. Importantly, His actions were consistently aligned with His declarations, showing that divine manifestation involves not just saying or planning but doing in harmony with one's words.

"For verily I say unto you, That whosoever shall say

unto this mountain, Be thou removed, and be thou cast into the sea; and shall not doubt in his heart, but shall believe that those things which he saith shall come to pass; he shall have whatsoever he saith." (Mark 11:23-24 KJV)

"Therefore I say unto you, What things soever ye desire, when ye pray, believe that ye receive them, and ye shall have them." (Mark 11:24 KJV)

These verses encapsulate the essence of the protocols of manifestation: vision, utterance, and concurring action. They encourage us to clearly visualize our desires, speak them with conviction, and align our actions to support what we declare. By following these divine steps, we engage the same creative process that God used at the foundation of the world, empowering us to transform our spiritual visions into physical realities.

Vision: The Catalyst For Hope And Faith

Vision holds a fundamental role in nurturing both hope and faith. In the spiritual journey, when our hope is anchored in the Word of God, faith inevitably begins to stir within us. This faith blossoms through hearing the Word and receiving personal affirmation that the promises of God are meant specifically for us. This affirmation marks the transition from mere belief to active faith, prompting us to visualize ourselves living out these promises.

Abraham's story is a quintessential example of faith's power, driven by vision against all odds. Despite his advanced age and Sarah's barrenness, Abraham clung to hope when there seemed no logical reason to do so. His hope was not unfounded but was based on a direct promise from God— a promise that was affirmed when God showed him the stars and declared his descendants would be just as numerous. This moment wasn't just an encouragement; it was an activation of Abraham's vision, helping him hold on to his faith even when doubts arose.

Activating Vision

The process of visualization is critical in the law of faith. To truly embrace what God has promised, we must vividly imagine it coming to pass. This mental imaging is a form of honoring God— it shows our trust and confidence in His word. Creating physical representations such as drawings or written descriptions can further solidify this vision, transforming God's promises from abstract concepts into concrete goals that occupy our minds and stir our spirits.

God's instructions to the Israelites as they received the law underscore the importance of keeping divine commands ever-present:

"And these words, which I command thee this day, shall be in thine heart: And thou shalt teach them diligently unto thy children, and shalt talk of them when thou sittest in thine house, and when thou walkest by the way, and when thou liest down, and when thou risest up. And thou shalt bind them for a sign upon thine hand, and they shall be as frontlets between thine eyes." (Deuteronomy 6:6-8 KJV)

These commands were meant to be a constant visual and mental presence, integrated into every aspect of daily life. The Israelites were to immerse themselves in the words of God, ensuring that these teachings were not only learned but lived. This immersion is a form of visualization, where the commandments become a lens through which they view the world and their choices.

The Importance Of Dreaming

Every believer is called to be a dreamer. Dreams are born from visions grounded in divine truth. They are not idle fantasies but are visions of what God has called us to manifest. Just as God commanded the Israelites to keep His words ever before them, believers today are called to keep their divine visions in constant view. This ongoing visualization not only aids in maintaining faith but also ensures that our actions align with our beliefs, thereby manifesting God's promises in our lives.

Developing a dream from visualizing hope is essential in exercising robust faith. By continually imagining and aligning our lives with God's promises, we not only honor Him but also activate the spiritual mechanisms that allow these promises to manifest in our lives. Let us then be diligent in nurturing our visions, for they are the seeds from which our faith grows and blossoms.

Utterance: Giving Voice To Vision

Utterance, or the articulation of our vision, plays a critical role in manifesting the dreams we hold. It's not enough to simply see with the eyes of faith; we must also speak with the voice of belief. The act of speaking breathes life into our visions, transforming them from internal contemplations to external realities.

As stated in 2 Corinthians 4:13, "We having the same spirit of faith, according as it is written, I believed, and therefore have I spoken; we also believe, and therefore speak." This scripture underscores the necessity of verbal expression in the faith journey. It is through speaking that we activate the spiritual and natural laws that govern the manifestation of our faith. Just as God spoke the universe into existence, we too are called to give voice to our visions. Without utterance, even the omnipotent power available at God's command would remain dormant; the universe would not have materialized from mere thought alone.

The importance of words in shaping our reality is further emphasized by Jesus in Matthew 12:37, "For by thy words thou shalt be justified, and by thy words thou shalt be condemned." This principle is mirrored in Romans 10:8-10, where Paul explains that salvation itself hinges on confession: "That if thou shalt confess with thy mouth the Lord Jesus, and shalt believe in thine heart that God hath raised him from the dead, thou shalt be saved. For with the heart man believeth unto righteousness; and with the mouth confession is made unto salvation." These passages illustrate that words are not merely descriptors but creators of our lived experience.

Engaging Words To Shape Reality

Using words to align our reality with our spiritual insights is incredibly powerful. When faced with circumstances that press a negative reality upon us, the act of speaking positive, faith-filled words can fortify our hearts and minds against despair. Words can literally shape our future; they can bring life or death, joy or sorrow, as reflected in Proverbs 18:21, "Death and life are in the power of the tongue: and they that love it shall eat the fruit thereof."

The Role Of Praise And Thanksgiving

Praise and thanksgiving are among the most potent forms of utterance. Psalms 22:3 tells us, "But thou art holy, O thou that inhabitest the praises of Israel." When we praise God, we invite His presence into our circumstances, effectively elevating our perception of Him above any adverse situation we might face. Similarly, thanksgiving is not just an act of gratitude but a declaration that challenges and overcomes misleading perceptions, aligning our reality with God's truth.

To effectively use utterance, start by aligning your words with God's promises. Speak them aloud regularly, not as a wishful thought, but as a declaration of what will manifest. When negative situations arise, counter them with spoken words of hope and faith based on scriptural truths, not mere appearances. Regularly engage in praise and thanksgiving to maintain an environment where God's presence feels near and His promises feel tangible.

In essence, the journey of faith is not silent; it is vocal and dynamic. It involves declaring with our mouths what we hold in our hearts, thereby setting the stage for the physical manifestation of our spiritual realities. Let us speak life into our circumstances, frame our world with our words, and watch as our divine visions materialize before our eyes.

Concurring Action: The Proof Of Faith

In the realm of faith, belief alone is not sufficient —action must follow. This principle underscores that faith, without tangible expression, is inert and ineffectual, akin to a body devoid of life. James 2:26 asserts, "For as the body without the spirit is dead, so faith without works is dead also." This vivid analogy compels us to examine the dynamic relationship between faith and action within our spiritual practices.

The Imperative Of Action In Faith

Faith necessitates concurring actions that substantiate the beliefs we profess. These actions are the evidence that our faith is alive, active, and poised to manifest the promises of God in our lives. The story of Abraham, referred to as the father of many nations, illustrates this beautifully. Despite the seeming impossibility due to their advanced ages, Abraham and Sarah embraced God's promise of a child. When God changed Abram's name to Abraham, which means "father of many nations," this wasn't just a symbolic act. It was an invitation for Abraham to align his actions with his new identity.

Abraham's response to God's promise wasn't passive. He didn't dismiss the promise due to the physical improbabilities but engaged actively with the promise. He and Sarah had marital relations, fully embracing the hope of a child and demonstrating their faith through their actions. This wasn't merely wishful thinking; it was hope put into action—hope that was rigorously tested yet emerged triumphant. Their steadfastness turned hope into reality, birthing Isaac and affirming the truth of God's word.

Similarly, the heroes of faith chronicled in Hebrews 11 shared a common trait: they acted in accordance with their faith. Moses is another prime example. He didn't just passively receive God's instructions; he acted on them. He confronted Pharaoh, led the Israelites out of Egypt, and approached the Red Sea not merely as a barrier but as a gateway to deliverance promised by God. His faith was not demonstrated by words alone but by stepping into the waters, staff in hand, trusting in God's promise of safety and passage.

Faith Manifested Through Actions

These actions—whether Abraham's acceptance of his new name and its implications, or Moses' confrontation with the sea—were not blind leaps into the dark but were steps taken in the full light of God's promises. They reflect a profound truth: real faith is never static or silent; it speaks and moves. It is faith that sees the invisible and believes the improbable, but it also acts on that belief, transforming the spiritual into the tangible.

Concurring action is essential for the manifestation of faith. It is the physical expression of our spiritual convictions. As we walk in faith, let us be mindful that our actions are powerful testimonies of the faith we hold. They are the practical demonstrations that our faith is not dead but vibrant and effective, capable of influencing realities and achieving divine purposes. Therefore, let our lives reflect our faith not only in what we believe but also in what we do, for faith without works is truly dead.

By Faith We Please God

God, the originator and perfecter of our faith, stands infallible. His Word remains steadfast, His power unparalleled. When God makes a promise, it is as good as done; when He decrees, it inevitably comes to fruition. Anchoring our faith in His declarations places us on firm, immovable ground. Unlike the ever-changing perspectives of humanity, our faith is built upon the solid rock of God's eternal assurances.

Navigating Life's Storms Through Faith

Life's journey is invariably marked by storms that test our resolve, challenge our beliefs, and stir our deepest fears. Yet, it is within these tumultuous times that our faith is not only tested but also fortified. Faith is far more than a passive state of acceptance—it is a dynamic engagement with the promises made by God. It provides solace for our hearts and strength to our hopes, enabling us to look past our immediate predicaments to the ultimate fulfillment of God's word.

When our faith is deeply rooted in the truth of Scripture, we become immovable despite the chaotic storms life may throw our way. Our foundation is secure, not because of our own capabilities, but because it is laid by the One who called us into being and is committed to bringing His good work in us to completion. This profound assurance is derived not from our own innate strength but from the Almighty Himself, who guarantees to sustain and uphold us.

Faith As Active Reliance On God

Engaging with God through faith means actively relying on His promises during both calm and crisis. It involves an ongoing dialogue with God, where we continually seek His strength and wisdom to navigate every aspect of our lives. This active faith solaces our hearts and fortifies our spirits, allowing us to transcend our circumstances and embrace the divine outcomes God has prepared for us.

Thus, by faith, we do not merely survive; we thrive. By trusting in the immovable and unchangeable nature of God's Word, we align ourselves with

His divine will, which transforms our trials into testimonies and our fears into victories. It is through this unwavering faith that we please God, demonstrating our complete trust in His sovereign power and loving providence. As we journey through life, let our faith be the beacon that guides us through darkness and into the glorious realization of His promises.

Living by faith transforms our existence into a vivid demonstration of the truths declared by God. It compels us to act, not merely as believers of the Word but as doers who base decisions on divine assurance rather than sensory evidence. This active faith is the force that relocates mountains, heals the sick, and actualizes God's promises in our daily lives.

Faith is more than a blind leap into unknown realms; it is a confident step into the well-lit path of God's truth. It operates on the principle that although our human eyes cannot discern the way forward, we are navigated by the omniscient Creator who knows our end from our beginning. This faith anchors not in fluctuating outcomes but in the steadfast nature and promises of God.

The Distinction Between Faith And Presumption

The key distinction between faith and presumption lies in their foundations; faith is underpinned by the spiritual realities of God's word. It is not a whimsical creation of the mind but a solid conviction rooted in the declaration that "God has spoken." Presumption, on the other hand, is often based on personal desires and logical deductions, devoid of divine endorsement.

Faith involves a dynamic interaction with the scriptures. It requires a heart attuned to the spiritual evidences provided by God, confirming His promises and His will. This interaction assures us that our actions, inspired by faith, are not mere gambles but calculated responses to God's revealed truth.

In practice, faith's potency is displayed in actions that seem contrary to natural laws but are aligned with divine principles. By faith, the sick are healed —not merely through wishful thinking, but through the invocative power of prayer that activates God's healing virtue. Mountains of difficulty are moved not by physical might but by the authoritative command in Jesus' name, rooted in the certainty of His will.

Faith As A Lifestyle

Thus, to live by faith is to live a life that visibly reflects God's promises through our every action. It is to walk daily in the assurance of His word, confronting challenges not with human strategies but with divine wisdom. Our journey of faith is marked by a series of steps taken in the light of God's assurances, each step a testament to our trust in His eternal character. In embracing this walk, we model a lifestyle that not only anticipates miracles but also creates a fertile environment for God's promises to flourish into reality.

Living by faith fundamentally alters our perception of life's challenges and difficulties. It shifts our perspective, encouraging us to see these trials not merely as obstacles, but as opportunities for God to manifest His faithfulness. This transformation teaches us to find joy not only in our present blessings but also in the eager anticipation of what God has promised to deliver. Our faith, thus, does not just navigate us through life—it becomes the mechanism by which we overcome the adversities of the world (1 John 5:4).

Faith As A Lens Of Victory

Faith equips us to view every challenge through the lens of victory. It is the evidence of things not seen, the assurance of things hoped for (Hebrews 11:1). This evidential faith guides us like a beacon through our darkest times, ensuring us that despite the blackest nights, the dawn is inevitable and God's promises are sure to be realized. In the midst of trials, our faith becomes more than just belief —it becomes the victory that transcends worldly constraints.

In our journey of faith, it is essential to steadfastly cling to this unseen evidence and assured hope. Faith provides us with the strength to persevere, the courage to keep believing when circumstances seem bleak, and the confidence that with God, all possibilities unfold. It empowers us to continue our paths, not with weary spirits but with renewed vigor, knowing that what we await in faith will manifest in God's perfect timing.

The call to live by faith, and not by sight (2 Corinthians 5:7), invites us to trust deeply in the reliability of God—the One who has initiated the good work within us and who is faithful to complete it (Philippians 1:6). This trust is not passive; it is an active, living faith that continually seeks to align every thought, action, and decision with God's will.

Embracing Life With Faith

By embracing life with faith, we unlock a new dimension of living. It is a life marked by a profound joy that transcends circumstances, fortified by the certainty that our future is securely held in God's capable hands. Living by faith allows us to enjoy each moment with a heart full of confidence and joy, regardless of the challenges we face.

Ultimately, faith is the key to truly loving life. It

compels us to embrace each moment, not with fear or uncertainty, but with the joyous assurance that comes from knowing our lives are woven intricately into the greater tapestry of God's divine plan. In faith, we find the strength to face the unknown, the grace to endure trials, and the hope that sustains our souls. Let us then journey forward with faith as our guide, celebrating each step taken in divine assurance, and each victory gained through our unwavering trust in God.

CHAPTER 5- LIVING BY LOVE

L ove, in its truest and most pure form, is not just an emotion but a profound expression of God's character manifested through us. It is the external flow of the divine qualities that reside within our hearts. When we love, we engage in an act of giving that transcends the mere exchange of material possessions. This giving involves the very essence of who we are—our time, our energy, and our compassion. Love compels us to recognize and nurture the potential we see in others, striving to ensure that it does not go to waste.

The Nature Of True Love

1 Corinthians 13:4-7 provides a clear depiction of love's attributes: "Love suffereth long, and is kind;

love envieth not; love vaunteth not itself, is not puffed up, doth not behave itself unseemly, seeketh not its own, is not provoked, taketh not account of evil; rejoiceth not in unrighteousness, but rejoiceth with the truth; beareth all things, believeth all things, hopeth all things, endureth all things."

These verses highlight that genuine love is outward-looking and other-centered. It is patient, kind, and devoid of envy. True love does not boast, nor is it proud. Rather, it is dignified, selfless, and calm under provocation. It does not dwell on wrongs but celebrates the truth. Love endures through difficulties, believes in the good, remains hopeful under challenging circumstances, and perseveres against all odds.

In our contemporary world, there is a pervasive lie that self-centeredness leads to happiness. This notion is often masked as "self-love," but true self-love is not self-centered. True self-value is demonstrated through usefulness and service to others. Just as a river must flow outward to remain fresh, so too must individuals give of themselves to experience genuine joy and fulfillment.

Living by love means actively deciding to embody the characteristics of divine love in all interactions and relationships. It challenges us to look beyond ourselves and to pour into others the love that we have received from God. In doing so, we not only enrich our own lives but also bring light and life to those around us, fulfilling the true purpose of love.

As we move forward in this chapter, let us explore the transformative power of living by love and how it can reshape our world and the lives of those we touch.

Giving As The Highest Act Of Love

Giving embodies the essence of love. It is an act that transcends the mere exchange of material goods, representing a deeper sharing of oneself. Rather than depleting our resources, giving strengthens our spiritual vitality, enhancing personal growth and fortification. In the words of Jesus:

"Give, and it shall be given unto you; good measure, pressed down, shaken together, and running over, shall men give into your bosom. For with the same measure that ye mete withal it shall be measured to you again." (Luke 6:38 KJV)

The term "agape," often translated as "charity" in the King James Version, underscores that giving is the ultimate expression of love. This concept is pivotal to understanding that giving not only benefits the recipient but also positions the giver to receive abundantly in return. This principle, known as the Law of Reciprocity, highlights that the generosity we extend to others will be returned to us in kind.

The Spiritual Law Of Giving

Jesus's teachings extend this principle even to our adversaries, advocating for benevolence towards those who oppose us. This act of giving can disarm adversaries and align them with the natural laws of life, reflecting wisdom similar to that of King Solomon:

"If thine enemy be hungry, give him bread to eat; and if he be thirsty, give him water to drink: For thou shalt heap coals of fire upon his head, and the LORD shall reward thee." (Proverbs 25:21-22 KJV)

Paul reiterates this in Romans, emphasizing that vengeance should be left to God, and we should instead overcome evil with good through acts of kindness.

Giving not only fosters external harmony but also promotes internal purification and health improvement. Luke 11:41 highlights that altruistic actions cleanse us spiritually: "But give for alms those things which are within; and behold, all things are clean unto you." This cleansing effect can have profound implications for personal tranquility and well-being.

Historical And Biblical Insights On Giving

From a historical perspective, even the spiritual advisements to monarchs, such as in the Book of Daniel, recommended generosity towards the vulnerable as a means to ensure peace and prolong prosperity:

"Wherefore, O king, let my counsel be acceptable unto thee, and break off thy sins by righteousness, and thine iniquities by showing mercy to the poor; if it may be a lengthening of thy tranquility." (Daniel 4:27 KJV)

This counsel suggests that charitable actions could extend the king's reign of peace and enhance his health.

Isaiah 58:7-8 further illuminates the benefits of giving, indicating that acts of charity can lead to personal rejuvenation and spiritual enlightenment: *"Is it not to deal thy bread to the hungry, and that thou bring the poor that are cast out to thy house? when thou seest the naked, that thou cover him; and that thou hide not thyself from thine own flesh? Then shall thy light break forth as the morning, and thine health shall spring forth speedily: and thy righteousness shall go before thee; the glory of the LORD shall be thy rearward."*

Thus, the power of giving is immense, extending beyond simple acts of kindness to profound impacts on our spiritual health, personal growth, and societal harmony. It is a divine principle that enriches both giver and receiver, fulfilling the scriptural promise that true generosity leads to abundant life. Let us embrace giving not only as a duty but as a privileged opportunity to manifest love, receive blessings, and experience the holistic healing that comes from selfless generosity.

Embracing The Spirit Of Generosity

Living by love entails weaving the spirit of giving into the very fabric of our daily lives. It involves extending our love not just to those immediately around us—our family and friends—but also to strangers, and even to the natural world that sustains us. Each act of kindness, whether big or small, each moment of care, and every gesture of generosity is a reflection of the divine love that God has instilled within us.

One of the core aspects of living by love is finding joy in the act of giving itself. This joy does not stem from anticipating rewards or public acknowledgment but rather from the deep fulfillment that comes from embodying love in our actions. Whether as a businessperson, a parent, a friend, or a neighbor, expressing love through our unique capabilities in our specific situations offers a richness that surpasses the fleeting satisfaction derived from material achievements.

Beyond Material Giving

It's crucial to understand that the essence of true love transcends the mere physical act of giving. While it's possible to offer material gifts without a genuine connection, authentic love demands a deeper engagement. True love involves giving from the heart—it means actively seeking the best for others and valuing their well-being as deeply as our own.

This type of love looks beyond the external needs of individuals and taps into their emotional and spiritual needs. When we interact with others, seeing them as fellow creations of God, our acts of kindness are imbued with greater meaning and purpose. The most significant expressions of love, therefore, share not only physical resources but also the intangible yet priceless gifts of care, attention, and compassion.

This approach to living by love enriches our lives in profound ways. By consistently practicing generosity and compassion, we create ripples of kindness that extend beyond our immediate circles. This not only enhances our personal sense of fulfillment but also contributes to a more loving and compassionate world.

In essence, living by love is about embedding the ethos of selfless giving into every interaction and decision. It's about making love a visible force in the world through our daily actions and relationships. As we cultivate this loving kindness, we not only align ourselves more closely with divine principles but also foster a community where love, care, and compassion flourish. This is living by love— transforming every opportunity into an act of grace that uplifts and inspires all who come into our sphere of influence.

Embracing Our Divine Purpose

Embracing our divine purpose is fundamentally about allowing love to permeate our hearts and actions. When love guides us, our primary concern becomes addressing and resolving the common challenges we face as a community. This selfless desire to solve problems for others acts as a catalyst, revealing and refining the unique gifts God has embedded within us—gifts meant to channel His divine power.

Each individual is endowed with a distinctive way through which God desires to manifest Himself. By accepting and embracing this divine calling, and allowing ourselves to become conduits of His love, we achieve our highest potential. It is through self-giving, in various forms that mirror God's love, that we truly embody the essence of living by love.

Living As Vessels Of Divine Love

Living by love serves as a powerful testament to God's glory. Every act of kindness, every gesture of giving, is both a reflection of His character and a manifestation of His love in the world. Through these acts, we do more than enrich our own lives; we profoundly impact the lives of others, extending

LOVING LIFE

God's love and glory far beyond our immediate reach.

Discovering Our True Gifts Through Service

Our truest gifts are often uncovered in the service of love. It is in the midst of our efforts to address the needs of others that our latent talents are honed and brought to light. This process of discovery and sharpening occurs not because we seek approval or accolades from those we help, but because we are aligned with God's purpose for us.

In serving others, we do not aim for their praise but seek the affirmation of God. Our greatest joy comes from knowing that we are valued by our Creator and that we are contributing meaningfully to His universal design. In this service, we find not only our true selves but also the deep satisfaction of playing an integral role in a larger cosmic scheme.

Ultimately, embracing our divine purpose through acts of love allows us to live fully realized lives that resonate with the rhythms of divine intent. It encourages us to shed the superficial layers of self-interest and dive deep into a life of genuine service and altruistic love. As we navigate this journey, we discover that our most profound fulfillment comes not from what we acquire, but from what we give and how well we reflect the love of God in our daily endeavors. This is the essence of living by love: to act as bearers of light and love in a world that desperately needs both.

Self Love Through Self-Discovery

True self-love is achieved through the journey of self-discovery, not through indulgence or material accumulation. Buying an array of material items or seeking pleasure in food and drink might bring temporary satisfaction, but they do not constitute genuine self-love. The real key to embracing self-love lies in identifying and nurturing one's unique role within the grand tapestry of life. Understanding and developing one's innate gifts is crucial to fostering a sense of self-worth.

Consider the process of refining gold. When gold is first mined, it appears unremarkable and its value is not readily apparent to the untrained eye. People may overlook it because its potential isn't obvious. However, once the gold is refined, its true beauty and worth are undeniable, attracting buyers willing to offer substantial sums of money for it.

This transformation mirrors the journey of self-discovery and development. True self-development isn't about adding more to ourselves—it's about stripping away the non-essential and the superficial to reveal the powerful essence hidden within. This process involves shedding negative traits and behaviors while enhancing and honing one's inherent talents through practical application and service.

Developing And Valuing One's Gifts

One clear indicator of a person's true gift is their passion for sharing it with others. This passion is often driven by love—love for the gift itself and love for the impact it can have on the world. It is this giving spirit, fueled by genuine love and passion, that marks true self-love. Moreover, it is through the expression of this gift that an individual becomes truly valued by others.

Just as refined gold becomes a sought-after commodity, a person who has fully embraced and developed their unique capabilities becomes highly valued and appreciated in their community and beyond. This value does not come from external validation but from the self-assurance and purpose derived from fully understanding and utilizing one's gifts.

Thus, self-love is fundamentally about self-discovery and personal growth. It involves digging deep to unearth one's true potential and diligently refining it to its purest form. Through this process, not only does one gain a profound appreciation for their intrinsic worth, but they also learn to love themselves in the most authentic and fulfilling way. This journey of self-love encourages a generous spirit, where one is driven to share their refined gifts with the world, enhancing not only their own lives but also the lives of others around them.

Honor Your Self

To honor oneself means to value and hold in high esteem the intrinsic worth imbued by the Creator. There is often a fine line between self-honor and pride, which can sometimes blur, leading to confusion. Pride involves elevating oneself beyond one's current state—an exaggeration of self-worth, while self-honor is about acknowledging and respecting the divine investments made into one's life by the infinite wisdom of the Creator.

Understanding Self-Honor

Self-honor requires a deep recognition of the gifts and potential that reside within one's soul. It's about treating oneself with the respect and care that these divine endowments deserve. Recognizing your unique qualities and capabilities isn't an act of pride but a foundation for gratitude. It allows you to appreciate the beauty within yourself—a beauty that even the heavenly hosts recognize and value.

Psalm 139:13-16 profoundly illustrates this concept:

"For thou hast possessed my reins: thou hast covered me in my mother's womb. I will praise thee; for I am fearfully and wonderfully made: marvellous are thy works; and that my soul knoweth right well. My substance was not hid from thee, when I was made in secret, and curiously wrought in the lowest parts of the earth. Thine eyes did see my substance, yet being unperfect; and in thy book all my members were written, which in continuance were fashioned, when as yet there was none of them."

This passage speaks to each of us, affirming that God was intimately involved in our creation from the very beginning. Despite the physical imperfections that might arise due to the corruption of creation, the value of one's soul remains unaltered in the eyes of God. He sees beyond the physical vessel to the soul within—a soul capable of radiating His glory regardless of external conditions.

The Value Of The Soul

God's estimation of us focuses on the soul, not the body. A powerful soul, residing in any type of body, can manifest divine glory and bring praise to its Creator. This understanding should elevate our self-respect and honor, as we are not just random assemblages of atoms but carefully crafted beings whose every detail has been recorded and cherished by God since conception.

Hence, honoring oneself is a sacred duty. It is about recognizing and valuing the divine craftsmanship that we are—fearfully and wonderfully made. When we honor what God has placed within us, we live in alignment with His purpose, expressing gratitude not just in words but through the very act of cherishing and nurturing the gifts He has given us. By doing so, we not only affirm our worth but also reflect the glory of our Creator in the most profound way.

PART THREE

THE WAY OF LIFE

CHAPTER 6-
LIVING LIFE NOW

Throughout our exploration in "Loving Life," we have delved deeply into the profound concepts of hope, faith, and love. As we transition to Chapter 6, entitled "Living Life Now," we are confronted with the compelling immediacy and urgency of life. This chapter serves as a reminder that life is a precious gift, not to be deferred or taken for granted but to be embraced and experienced fully in the here and now.

The Deception Of Tomorrow

In the journey of life, one of the most pervasive deceptions is the belief in the ever-present 'tomorrow' as a better opportunity for actions we delay today. This notion of perpetual tomorrows not only breeds procrastination but also frequently results in missed opportunities and unrealized potential.

James 4:13-15 provides a profound reflection on the uncertainty and fleeting nature of life:

"Go to now, ye that say, To day or to morrow we will go into such a city, and continue there a year, and buy and sell, and get gain: Whereas ye know not what shall be on the morrow. For what is your life? It is even a vapour, that appeareth for a little time, and then vanisheth away. For that ye ought to say, If the Lord will, we shall live, and do this, or that."

This scripture poignantly illustrates that life is like vapor—present one moment and gone the next. It challenges us to acknowledge the fragility and unpredictability of our existence and the folly in postponing crucial decisions or actions to a future that is not guaranteed. The key is not to miss any moment of one's life, but to make the most of every moment. Tomorrow builds on today, a beautiful tomorrow is only a seed sown by maximizing today.

The Risks Of Procrastination

Procrastinating on today's responsibilities by banking on tomorrow is not only risky but often diminishes the joy and potential embedded in the present. It's a common trap that denies us the full experience and satisfaction of living in the "now." In theological terms, it reflects a misalignment from the will of God, who calls us to seize the opportunities of the present rather than deferring them indefinitely.

"Behold, now is the accepted time; behold, now is the day of salvation," (2 Corinthians 6:2) reminds us. This directive emphasizes the immediacy of action required in our spiritual and secular lives, underscoring that the only moment truly in our control and guaranteed to us is the present.

Moreover, dwelling on the past can be as debilitating as fixating on the future. While the past can offer valuable lessons, it should not shackle us with its failures or nightmares. Each new day should be approached as a fresh opportunity, not weighed down by yesterday's errors. Employing hope as a shield can protect us from the paralysis that past disappointments often bring.

Living Vibrantly Today

Every day is a unique gift and should be lived with as much vigor and earnestness as if it were the only day we have. This perspective encourages us to live fully and intensely—loving without hesitation, giving generously, and embracing both the joys and challenges of the moment without reservations.

Adopting this approach transforms how we interact with the world and with ourselves. It compels us to act now, love now, and live now, with the understanding that the present is our most valuable possession. Let us then step boldly into each day with a heart ready to act upon our divine calling, mindful that in the grand design of eternity, today is all we can truly claim.

Making The Most Of Now

Making the most of the present involves a full engagement with our immediate circumstances—valuing our relationships, pursuing our passions, and fulfilling our duties with vigor and commitment. It means liberating ourselves from the constraints of past regrets and the worries of future uncertainties. Living in the "now" enables us to concentrate our efforts on impactful actions today, appreciate the mundane moments that weave together the tapestry of our daily existence, and uncover joy in the seemingly small things.

Our journey through life is frequently obstructed by two profound time wasters: dwelling on what has been and fretting over what might be. Embracing the present requires us to release the sorrows of yesterday and the anxieties of tomorrow. This approach doesn't imply that we dismiss the past or disregard the future. Instead, it involves drawing lessons from past experiences and making informed plans for the future, all while maintaining our primary focus on the present.

Living In The Present

To truly live in the now, we need to practice letting go of these distractions. This means intentionally forgetting the mistakes and hurts of the past—not letting them dictate our current emotional state —and not allowing the uncertainty of the future to paralyze our actions today. By focusing on the present, we are more likely to respond proactively to the opportunities that arise, and we become better equipped to handle challenges with grace and resilience.

By concentrating on the present, we open ourselves to the richness and fullness of life that God has designed for us. This involves appreciating every moment, recognizing the potential in the ordinary, and understanding that our most profound joy often results from fully engaging with the here and now. We are called not just to pass through life but to live it fully, to soak in the vast array of experiences it offers, and to cherish the journey as much as the destination.

Living life now doesn't just enhance our own well-being; it enriches our interactions with others, deepens our personal growth, and amplifies our impact on the world around us. It's about making a conscious choice to live deliberately and purposefully, day by day, moment by moment. As we shift our focus to the present, we find that life's true essence unfolds before us, offering a path filled with vibrancy and possibility. Let's embrace this path with open hearts and find joy in the abundance of the present moment.

Living In The Present: A Daily Practice

To truly "live life now" is to embrace each day as a precious gift from God—a gift to be unwrapped, cherished, and fully enjoyed. This approach calls for an active engagement with life, a deep appreciation for the blessings we currently enjoy, and a dedicated effort to utilize our God-given talents to positively impact the world. Living this way means embracing life with purpose, passion, and praise, and recognizing that every moment offers an opportunity to glorify God through our actions, relationships, and our very existence.

Living life now is more than a philosophical concept; it's a daily practice. It's an invitation to immerse ourselves in the richness of life, to love deeply, act justly, and walk humbly with our God, as Micah 6:8 advises. We must remember that the time to live, love, and make a difference is not some distant tomorrow but today. Therefore, we should approach each day with the joy, urgency, and purpose that comes from understanding that life is happening right now.

The Importance Of Small Actions

Living life to the fullest doesn't necessarily mean making grand gestures every day. Often, it's the small, consistent acts that align with who we are meant to be that bring the most joy and fulfillment. Consider dedicating time each day—even just an hour—to nurture and express the best of what lies within you. This daily investment can transform your life more profoundly than sporadic grand actions.

My understanding of living in the present once led me to a simple yet life-changing action. I realized that I possessed a wealth of content that could bless others, yet I was held back by my poor self-image. While reflecting on this in my room one day, I noticed something as mundane as my wardrobe. It struck me that while clothes might seem trivial, they play a crucial role in how we perceive ourselves and project that image to the world.

I decided then to make a change. I began to replace any clothing that didn't align with the positive image I wanted to project. This wasn't about pleasing others but about affirming my self-worth and aligning my external environment with my internal aspirations.

Daily Habits And Personal

Transformation

The way we dress, our posture, and even our routine movements contribute to our subconscious self-image. By examining and adjusting these daily habits, we can start to tell our own story more accurately through our actions and presentation. If our daily routine doesn't reflect who we are—or who we aspire to be—it's crucial to develop or edit these aspects of our personal culture.

Every day, we have the opportunity to shape our identity and influence our world through small but meaningful decisions. Let's commit to living each day with intention and integrity, fully aware that the most significant changes often come from the smallest consistent actions. Let us embrace each day with the resolve to be our best selves, offering what we have and are to the service of both God and humanity. This is how we truly live life now—fully engaged, deeply connected, and passionately alive.

CHAPTER 7-
PEACE: THE MOST
NEEDED ASSET

Peace is crucial, not just nice to have. It's tied deeply to our human nature, embedded within the very fabric of who we are. But here's the thing—seeking peace isn't just about managing external chaos; it's an internal battle, too. Relying solely on ourselves to find peace is like running in circles; we end up right where we started, mainly because we're inherently flawed. Albert Einstein once pointed out that "It is easier to denature plutonium than to denature the evil spirit of man." If that doesn't put the challenge into perspective, what will?

The Trouble Within

Einstein's words shine a light on a hard truth: the darkness within us isn't easy to shake off. This inner evil, a hangover from humanity's fall from grace, keeps us from the divine peace we were meant to enjoy. When we decided to go it alone and step out of the Creator's plan, we didn't just lose a rulebook; we lost a part of ourselves—inviting a spirit of corruption that's been a thorn in our side ever since, killing our vibe and filling our lives with endless strife.

The Original Misstep

Let's rewind to the beginning—Genesis spells it out pretty clearly. When humanity opted for independence from God, we didn't just wander out of a garden; we walked away from peace and harmony themselves. That single act of defiance brought chaos into our lives and turned even the natural world, which we were supposed to look after, into a source of fear and anxiety.

Ever wonder why life often feels like an uphill battle? Why things like sickness, war, and natural calamities seem to follow us around? These aren't just random bouts of bad luck; they're reminders of what we've lost—our rightful place in the order of things. All these challenges strip away our peace, showing just how out of sync we are with the world.

Getting Back To Basics

Here's the kicker: peace with God is the bedrock of peace with everything else. Our split from the divine isn't just about missing Sunday school; it has real, tangible effects on our day-to-day life. It messes with our relationships, our environment, and that inner calm we all crave. Trying to patch things up without addressing our core disconnect is like trying to fill a sieve with water—it's futile.

Acknowledging that we can't manufacture peace on our own is a start. True peace needs a fix from the foundation up, reconnecting us with the divine. As we dig into this disconnect and its impact, there's a light at the end of the tunnel. Finding peace isn't about conquering the external mess or mastering life's many hurdles; it's about making amends with the Creator. This reunion doesn't just bring personal peace; it has the power to mend the deep-seated rifts tearing us apart from each other and from nature. Restoring this connection is our ticket to a peaceful existence, enabling us to live fully in the grand design intended for us.

Understanding Shalom

When we talk about divine peace, or "shalom" as

it's known in Hebrew, we're not just referring to a sense of calm or quiet. Shalom encompasses so much more—it includes prosperity, health, safety, and the fulfillment of all desires. It's about complete satisfaction, covering every aspect of life. So, when a Hebrew greets another with "Shalom," they're essentially wishing them every element necessary for a fully satisfied life. This expansive definition underscores why achieving this kind of peace on our own is a tall order. Economic theories teach us that human wants are insatiable, suggesting that the true peace we seek—the kind that satisfies completely on physical, spiritual, and emotional levels—is beyond what human efforts can provide.

The Nature Of The Creator

Divine peace isn't just a noble quality; it's the very essence of the Creator. In the Bible, God is referred to as Jehovah Shalom, which means "God is peace." This title reveals a profound truth: where there is peace, there God is present. Just as John the Apostle wrote that God is love, He is also the embodiment of peace. Peace, by its nature, harmonizes and binds together—it is inseparable from love, much like twins.

Reflecting on childhood, I recall moments of unexpected silence when we would whisper, "an angel just passed by." Looking back, these playful thoughts might not have been far off. Divine presence does indeed bring a palpable peace that is almost tangible. When God's presence is near, there is an overwhelming sense of peace that cannot be resisted.

This peace originates from God and is a fundamental aspect of His nature. An excellent illustration of this is found in the story of Gideon at the threshing floor (Judges 6:11-24). When the angel of the Lord appeared to Gideon with a message about leading Israel into battle, the departure of the angel in a supernatural manner revealed to Gideon that he had been in the presence of the divine. Despite the ancient belief that no one could see God and live, Gideon was not met with death but with peace—underscored by the angel's parting words of peace.

Divine peace, therefore, is not merely about the absence of conflict or the silence of solitude; it is about experiencing the comprehensive and harmonizing presence of God that satisfies the deepest desires of the spirit, soul, and body. This peace is a testament to the divine nature, offering a glimpse into the tranquil and profound serenity that aligns us with God's perfect will and presence.

Peace Amidst The Storm

First off, this peace is specifically *the peace of God*—you can't find it just anywhere; it's only present in God Himself. It's a direct manifestation of God's presence. We're not just talking about simple stillness or mere calm here. This peace is a comprehensive package that includes many blessings from God, such as prosperity and eternal glory. While the world might mimic this peace, it can never replicate the divine peace that Jesus spoke about:

"Peace I leave with you, my peace I give unto you: not as the world gives, do I give to you. Let not your heart be troubled, neither let it be afraid." (John 14:27 KJV)

This divine peace is what Jesus carried with Him, even in the face of natural and supernatural crises. It's the kind of peace He demonstrated on a stormy sea, recorded in Luke 8:22-24. While His disciples panicked, Jesus slept soundly in the boat. When they woke Him in desperation, He simply rebuked the wind and the raging waters, showcasing His mastery over life's tumults. Jesus was never confused, troubled, or fearful, regardless of the circumstances. He embodied the serene confidence that comes from knowing exactly what to do at any given moment.

This peace that Jesus refers to isn't about avoiding challenges or escaping problems; it's about facing them head-on with a heart untroubled by the outcome. It's a peace that transcends human understanding and situations, anchoring us firmly in the divine even amid life's storms. This is the peace that marks the true presence of God—a peace so profound that it can calm the mightiest storms, not just outside but within our hearts as well.

Peace Brings The Miraculous

The peace of God doesn't just soothe; it opens doors to the miraculous, unlocking the supernatural realm. Within this divine peace, we find the living faith—God's own faith—which we embrace boldly as we rest in the Lord's serene presence. This was the same peace at work when Jesus miraculously multiplied two fish and five loaves to feed thousands.

Unlike His followers, who were anxious about their apparent scarcity, Jesus maintained an extraordinary confidence in His heavenly Father. Had any of the disciples been asked to bless the food, they might have fallen back on routine prayers in a desperate bid to curry favor with God. But for Jesus, no such efforts were necessary. He understood something fundamental: the Father was already poised to act, all that was required was a thankful heart and faith, rooted in the unshakeable peace He shared with God.

This peace transcends mere calm; it is an active, dynamic presence that facilitates miracles by aligning us perfectly with God's will. Through this peace, we too can learn to trust in God's provision and timing, unleashing the miraculous in our lives.

Peace That Passes All Understanding

This peace, the kind that God gives, transcends all understanding. It goes far beyond what can be achieved through mental training or practices like yoga. It's not about psychological well-being; it's wholly spiritual. This peace doesn't rely on positive thinking or any mental gymnastics—it's beyond all that. It's a divine gift that flows directly from God's presence.

Moreover, this peace baffles those who witness it because it can't be rationalized with physical explanations. It typically shows its true strength in situations that seem insurmountable, in moments where there appears to be no way out. This is when its divine nature is most apparent, making it clear that such profound peace is the work of God, not humans. This is the peace that showcases God's supreme power, demonstrating that He, and He alone, is the source of true serenity.

God Dwells In Peace

God embodies peace not only as a trait but as His very environment.

"For the kingdom of God is not meat and drink; but righteousness, and peace, and joy in the Holy Ghost." (Romans 14:17 KJV)

In God's kingdom, peace is paramount, and to walk with Him, we must actively pursue it. We connect best with God when we are at peace, a state optimal for divine communication where God can infuse us with His virtues. Peace is the conduit through which we receive divine wisdom and it serves as a critical tool for discernment, helping us distinguish between divine guidance and deceitful interference.

A Personal Encounter

Let me share a personal experience that illustrates this. One day, I was reading a digital book from my collection, authored by someone advocating for mental healing techniques. As I read, I slipped into an experience I can describe as neither trance nor dream. I found myself in a stunning garden, surrounded by vibrant flowers and a refreshing fragrance, seemingly a slice of heaven.

A figure appeared before me, possessing the beauty of a woman and the form of a man—initially thought to be an angel. Yet, despite the allure, I felt uneasy; there was no peace. Upon regaining full consciousness, a clear message resonated within my spirit: "They have a form of beauty but there is no peace in them." This revelation helped me understand that what I encountered was a manifestation from the kingdom of darkness, not the divine.

The Bible warns us of such deceptions: "And no

marvel; for Satan himself is transformed into an angel of light." (2 Corinthians 11:14 KJV)

To avoid falling prey to such trickery, we need to employ discernment, where peace plays an essential role. The Holy Spirit often uses peace as a signpost, guiding us towards what is right. In moments of uncertainty, when trying to discern God's will, it's crucial to examine the peace within our hearts.

The Peace Test

If judgments remain unclear, the "peace test" becomes a vital tool. The option that brings tranquility to your inner being is likely the correct path. This inner peace, a hallmark of God's presence, is our most reliable indicator, ensuring that we align with God's will and avoid the snares set by the enemy.

Thus, in our quest for divine guidance, let us seek that peace which transcends all understanding, anchoring our decisions and illuminating our paths.

Sin carries a heavy price tag: death. The Scripture is clear that the wages of sin is death, and since humanity embodies this sinful nature, there is an inherent fear and anticipation of decay and death. Despite efforts to stave off this inevitable end, decay persists and worsens. This reality was vividly portrayed when Gideon encountered the divine presence in Judges 6. His immediate fear was death, a common human reaction when sinful nature comes face-to-face with divinity, typically resulting in divine judgment.

However, a significant moment unfolds in this narrative: "And the Lord said unto him, Peace be unto thee; fear not: thou shalt not die." (Judges 6:23)

Through a simple declaration of peace, Gideon was spared from death. This instance beautifully illustrates that even though humanity deserves death due to our sinful nature, God's declaration of peace offers protection and grace. It is through divine peace that we experience the grace of God.

Christ: Our Peace

This concept is further elaborated in the New Testament. Christ's mission was to bring peace through His sacrifice, bridging the gap between humanity and God: "But now in Christ Jesus ye who sometimes were far off are made nigh by the blood of Christ. For he is our peace, who hath made both one, and hath broken down the middle wall of partition between us; having abolished in his flesh the enmity, even the law of commandments contained in ordinances; for to make in himself of twain one new man, so making peace; and that he might reconcile both unto God in one body by the cross, having slain the enmity thereby: and came and preached peace to you which were afar off, and to them that were nigh. For through him we both have access by one spirit unto the Father." (Ephesians 2:13-18)

"And having made peace through the blood of his cross, by him to reconcile all things unto himself; by him, I say, whether they be things in earth, or things in heaven." (Colossians 1:20)

The Transformative Power Of Christ's Peace

Christ's peace did more than calm storms or soothe fears; it fundamentally changed our position before God. Through His death, Christ dismantled the barriers erected by sin and law, uniting us with God in a profound and holy reconciliation. This peace ensures that we are no longer distant or disparate from God but can approach His presence freely and without fear.

Without the peace brought by Christ, the Holy Spirit's arrival among us could have had catastrophic consequences, given the spirit's nature to enact judgment and uphold righteousness. Christ's peace was essential, preconditioning our hearts and spirits to receive the Holy Spirit without the fear of immediate death due to our inherent sinfulness.

In conclusion, peace is not just a tranquil state of mind but a life-saving gift from God, brought into the world through Christ. It delivers us from the ultimate consequence of sin—death—and grants us unhindered access to divine presence, transforming our relationship with God and each other. Through this peace, we live in the reassurance and grace that only God can provide.

Divine Peace Unveiled

"Glory to God in the highest, and on earth peace, goodwill toward men." (Luke 2:14 KJV)

This proclamation encapsulates the divine peace accessible only through a profound revelation. Belief and acceptance of this truth immediately open the door to unparalleled peace. This peace isn't just about stillness; it's about restoration and unity with God, regained through Jesus Christ. Once alienated by sin and shrouded in the darkness of this world, we struggled without rest, distant from the peace that passes all understanding.

Historically, humanity has sought to bridge this divide through religious rites, mistakenly believing that peace with God could be earned through offerings and sacrifices:

"Seven days shalt thou prepare every day a goat for a sin offering: they shall also prepare a young bullock, and a ram out of the flock, without blemish. Seven days shall they purge the altar and purify it; and they shall consecrate themselves..." (Ezekiel 43:25-27 KJV)

Yet, these efforts, while sincere, only scratched the surface. They could not forge the deep union with God that erases all traces of fear and separation, nor could they provide the peace that embeds confidence before the Creator.

God's Solution: Incarnation And Reconciliation

Understanding humanity's limitations, God enacted a profound plan of reconciliation through Christ. By becoming flesh, Christ bridged the eternal divide, offering Himself as the ultimate peace offering:

"And, having made peace through the blood of his cross, by him to reconcile all things unto himself; by him, I say, whether they be things in earth, or things in heaven." (Colossians 1:20 KJV)

Through His sacrifice, Christ did not just reconcile mankind but all creation, sanctifying us through His blood and granting us a new spirit.

Christ's triumph over the forces of chaos is celebrated:

"And having spoiled principalities and powers, he made a show of them openly, triumphing over them in it." (Colossians 2:15 KJV)

In defeating these powers, Christ didn't just win a battle; He secured our peace and eternal rest in Him. We are now overcomers through faith, assured of our salvation and a glorious future.

Living In Christ's Peace

The peace that Christ offers goes beyond mere tranquility; it is an active, dynamic force that reconciles, restores, and transforms. By His stripes, we are healed and brought into a new existence:

"But he was wounded for our transgressions, he was bruised for our iniquities: the chastisement of our peace was upon him; and with his stripes we are healed." (Isaiah 53:5 KJV)

This message of peace declares us free from our past transgressions and present iniquities. Christ's suffering was a divine exchange—He took on our pain and gave us His peace.

A New Creation In Christ

This peace ensures that we no longer see ourselves through the lens of our old selves but as new creations in Christ—spiritually reborn, distinct from our former selves, and intimately united with God. Our awareness of this spiritual rebirth fosters a profound peace, knowing that God no longer sees our flaws but the righteousness of Christ in us.

By embracing this peace, we live out our days in confidence and hope, continually affirming our union with Christ and celebrating the freedom His sacrifice has secured. This is not just a message; it's a transformation—a call to live as new creatures, forever at peace with God.

Peace For Spiritual Victory

It's a common lament: so much preaching, so many preachers, yet minimal impact on the people. This isn't because God's power to save or heal has diminished, but rather, the devil, the prince of ignorance, has succeeded in blinding our understanding. Many preach with good intentions, delivering messages that sound correct and biblically sound, yet they fall short of preaching the transformative gospel of Christ—the true power unto salvation.

While motivational preaching has its place, it lacks the salvific power to rescue a soul. Others focus intensely on divine retribution, hellfire, and the promise of heaven, or get caught up in the minutiae of dietary laws, clothing, and holy days, all of which perish with use. These messages, rather than revealing the Savior, can obstruct the seeker's view of the Lord of salvation.

When Jesus began His ministry, He could have addressed countless topics. Instead, He chose to focus squarely on the Kingdom of God:

"From that time Jesus began to preach, and to say, Repent: for the kingdom of heaven is at hand." (Matthew 4:17 KJV)

He instructed His disciples to do likewise, ensuring the consistency and purity of the message:

"And as ye go, preach, saying, the kingdom of heaven is at hand." (Matthew 10:7 KJV)

Their adherence to this directive allowed God's power to manifest through them, resulting in tangible, miraculous results.

Before ascending, Jesus crystallized this mission:

"And that repentance and remission of sins should be preached in his name among all nations, beginning at Jerusalem." (Luke 24:47 KJV)

This wasn't just for His first followers but for all believers throughout all ages. The essence of the gospel is about reconciling humanity back to God, sowing seeds of peace, and proclaiming divine forgiveness.

The Reality Of Spiritual Warfare

Our battle against the forces of darkness is fundamentally a fight of faith—striving to align human hearts with God. The devil employs guilt and unbelief to estrange people from the Lord. A heart devoid of peace is barricaded against divine blessings, despite God's readiness to reside within all who believe in Christ.

Today's teachings on spiritual warfare often miss the mark, emphasizing human efforts and thereby playing into the devil's hands. They inadvertently support the kingdom of darkness by perpetuating ignorance and elevating carnal desires.

Divine Strategy For Victory

The true nature of spiritual warfare is illuminated by the peace that only God can provide:

"The Lord shall fight for you, and ye shall hold your peace." (Exodus 14:14 KJV)

When we preach the gospel of peace—forgiveness of sins—we not only invite God's presence but also displace demonic influences. God doesn't delight in human might but in those who rest in His grace.

By preaching peace, we facilitate the manifestation of God's kingdom on earth, effectively dispelling darkness. Peace, love, and joy are inseparable elements of God's kingdom—each component supporting and amplifying the others. In their presence, demonic forces are neutralized, and God's sovereignty is affirmed.

The Call To Action

Our role is not to engage in frantic spiritual battles but to apply and direct the victorious power Christ has already secured. Wherever darkness rears its head, we are to bring the light of Christ's peace, ensuring that God's will prevails. This is the gospel of peace: a divine invitation to witness the transformative power of Christ, enabling us to live as victors in a world ensnared by spiritual darkness. Let us then move forward in this knowledge, confidently declaring the forgiveness and peace only found in Jesus Christ.

CONCLUSION-INTEGRATING HOPE, FAITH, LOVE, AND PEACE INTO DAILY LIVING

As we draw this exploration to a close, we have delved deeply into the essential spiritual principles that guide a fulfilling life: hope, faith, love, and importantly, peace. These elements are not isolated; they are deeply interconnected, each enhancing and supporting the others in the pursuit of a life that fully embraces both God's promises and our potential as human beings. This concluding chapter aims to synthesize these elements, providing a cohesive guide to embodying them in our daily lives.

The Symbiosis Of Hope, Faith, Love, And Peace

Hope sets the foundation, providing us with the forward-looking vision that fuels our daily pursuits. It is the anticipation of good that keeps us grounded yet aspirational, amid life's unpredictability. Hope is the confident expectation that no matter the current darkness, light is just around the horizon.

Faith builds upon this hope, offering a robust framework through which our aspirations can manifest into reality. It is the actionable step towards realizing the visions that hope sketches in our hearts. Faith involves trusting in the unseen promises of God, believing that His words are true, and acting in accordance with this belief—even when external circumstances have yet to change.

Love is the ultimate expression of what it means to live out our faith and hope. It is the active demonstration of both, through our interactions and commitments to others. Love compels us to put our faith into action and to endure in hope. It moves us beyond self-centered existences to serve, to give, and to cherish others in a pure reflection of God's love for us.

Peace is the tranquil backbone of this trio, providing

a calm and steady base from which hope, faith, and love can flourish. It is not merely the absence of conflict, but the presence of a serene assurance that God is in control. Peace allows us to withstand life's storms with a quiet confidence and to extend this stability to others in their times of turmoil.

Living Each Day With Purpose

To live by these principles means more than just understanding them; it requires their daily application. Each day offers new challenges and opportunities, but also a new canvas on which to paint our responses shaped by hope, faith, love, and peace.

In this part of our journey, let's clarify the difference between spirituality and religiosity. Often, people confuse becoming more religious with being more spiritual. However, spirituality involves connecting with God's realm directly through our spirit. It's about our relationship with God as a child and him as the father when we identify with Jesus Christ and become spiritually reborn.

On the other hand, religiosity focuses on performing specific rituals or acts to please God. But in Christianity, we understand that God is already pleased with us through our faith in Christ, not through the rituals we perform. As we grow in our spiritual life, we find that it is not about adhering to religious norms but about deepening this profound, spiritual connection with God. This growth brings us true peace.

Becoming To Manifest

The principle of spirituality is that you become before you manifest, this is why you must be diligent to employ this spiritual wisdom to maintain the picture that God is giving you through the scripture as you meditate. Refuse to accept false images do all you can to avoid negative images contrary to what God says about you.

Living a life guided by these principles is not without its challenges. It requires courage to hope when situations seem bleak, steadfastness to maintain faith when outcomes are uncertain, resilience to love when it is easier to be indifferent, and patience to remain peaceful amidst chaos. However, the rewards of such a life are immeasurable. Not only does it bring internal peace and satisfaction, but it also makes a tangible difference in the lives of others and glorifies God in the most authentic manner possible.

Conclusion

In conclusion, as we integrate hope, faith, love, and peace into our daily walk, we transform not only our own lives but also influence those around us in profound ways. These principles beckon us to rise above the mundane and the immediate, to touch the divine, and to participate in the eternal. Let us then move forward with a renewed commitment to live fully, love deeply, believe fervently, and remain peacefully centered. Let every day be a living testament to the truth that the best way to love life is to live it—one hopeful, faithful, loving, and peaceful step at a time.

ABOUT THE AUTHOR

Obiora Eze

About the author

Obiora Eze is a dedicated servant of God, whose life's work has been to illuminate the spiritual wisdom of Christ to all who cross his path. With a profound calling to teach, Obiora has devoted himself to sharing God's Word in roles that span from being a cherished children's teacher to serving with humility as a pastor and church planter. His journey in faith is marked by a tireless commitment to outreach, where he has been instrumental in leading countless individuals to a faith-filled and joyous walk with God.

Married and blessed with three children, Obiora resides in the United Kingdom, a place he now calls home and the current focus of his mission to spread hope. His approach to ministry is characterized by a deep understanding of the Scriptures, combined with a genuine love for people and a passion to see lives transformed through the knowledge and love of Jesus Christ.

Obiora's teachings resonate with people from all walks of life, offering them practical insights into living a life of peace, purpose, and deep spiritual fulfillment. His experiences as a pastor and church planter have endowed him with a rich perspective on the challenges and triumphs of faith, making his message both relatable and deeply inspiring.

In "Loving Life," Obiora Eze draws upon his extensive experience and personal journey of faith to offer readers a guide to finding true peace in a tumultuous world. Through this book, he extends an invitation to explore the principles and wisdom that guarantee a fulfilled life, a life that can be enjoyed without regrets.

Obiora's life and ministry are a testament to the power of faith in action. Through his work, he continues to spread a message of hope and peace, touching the lives of many and inspiring a new generation to walk in the joy and freedom that comes from a relationship with God.

Made in the USA
Columbia, SC
07 June 2024

36796602R00064